MW00966466

Welcome to
SCOTLAND

Gareth Stevens Publishing
A WORLD ALMANAC EDUCATION GROUP COMPANY

Written by
GRAEME CANE/LISE HULL

Edited in USA by
DOROTHY L. GIBBS

Designed by
GEOSLYN LIM

Picture research by
SUSAN JANE MANUEL

First published in North America in 2002 by
Gareth Stevens Publishing
A World Almanac Education Group Company
330 West Olive Street, Suite 100
Milwaukee, Wisconsin 53212 USA

Please visit our web site at:
www.garethstevens.com
For a free color catalog describing
Gareth Stevens Publishing's list of high-quality books
and multimedia programs, call
1-800-542-2595 or
fax your request to (414) 332-3567.

All rights reserved. No parts of this book may be reproduced or
utilized in any form or by any means electronic or mechanical,
including photocopying, recording, or by an information storage and
retrieval system, without permission from the copyright owner.

© **TIMES MEDIA PRIVATE LIMITED 2002**
Originated and designed by
Times Editions
an imprint of Times Media Private Limited
Times Centre, 1 New Industrial Road
Singapore 536196
http://www.timesone.com.sg/te

Library of Congress Cataloging-in-Publication Data
Cane, Graeme.
Welcome to Scotland / Graeme Cane and Lise Hull.
p. cm. — (Welcome to my country)
Summary: Presents information on the geography, history, government
and economy, arts, people, and social life and customs of Scotland.
Includes bibliographical references and index.
ISBN 0-8368-2539-X (lib. bdg.)
1. Scotland—Juvenile literature. [1. Scotland.]
I. Hull, Lise. II. Title. III. Series.
DA762.C37   2002
941.1—dc21   2001057802

Printed in Malaysia

1 2 3 4 5 6 7 8 9 06 05 04 03 02

PICTURE CREDITS
Heimo Aga/Globe Press: 3 (top), 23, 40
Art Directors and Trip Photo Library: cover,
   1, 6, 17, 18, 19, 22, 24, 25, 26, 31, 32,
   33, 34, 35, 36, 37 (both), 41, 43, 45
Bes Stock: 4, 8, 28
B.T.A.: 3 (center), 3 (bottom), 21, 39
Camera Press: 5, 9, 14, 16, 27
Hulton Getty/Archive Photos: 10, 12, 13,
   15 (center), 15 (bottom), 29 (right)
North Wind Picture Archives: 11, 29 (left)
Photobank Photolibrary: 2, 7, 20
Topham Picturepoint: 15 (top), 30, 38

Digital Scanning by Superskill Graphics Pte Ltd

Contents

5 **Welcome to Scotland!**

6 **The Land**

10 **History**

16 **Government and the Economy**

20 **People and Lifestyle**

28 **Language**

30 **Arts**

34 **Leisure**

40 **Food**

42 **Map**

44 **Quick Facts**

46 **Glossary**

47 **Books, Videos, Web Sites**

48 **Index**

Words that appear in the glossary are printed in **boldface** type the first time they occur in the text.

Welcome to Scotland!

"A hundred thousand welcomes" is a Gaelic (GAY-lik) greeting often heard in Scotland. The Scots are famous for their friendliness. They are also very loyal to their homeland, which, today, is part of the United Kingdom. Let's visit this fascinating country and learn more about the friendly Scots.

Opposite: Street performers entertain shoppers in Edinburgh, the capital of Scotland.

Below: These boys are wearing kilts, which are traditional dress for men and boys in Scotland.

The Flag of Scotland

Scotland's official flag has a white, x-shaped cross on a blue background. It is the cross of Saint Andrew. A legend says that, during an ancient battle, clouds in the sky shaped like this cross predicted victory for the Scots.

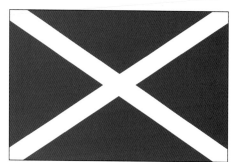

The Land

Scotland covers about one-third of the island of Great Britain. Like England, Wales, and Northern Ireland, it is part of the United Kingdom. England is south of Scotland, the Atlantic Ocean is to the north and west, and the North Sea is to the east. The country has 787 islands, but only 130 of them are **inhabited**. The Hebrides, the Orkneys, and the Shetlands are Scotland's main island groups.

Below: In the Central Lowlands, winding rivers and green fields provide breathtaking views.

Scotland has three main land areas: the Highlands in the north, the Central Lowlands, and the Southern Uplands. The Highlands have many lakes and mountains. In the Grampian Mountains, Ben Nevis, at 4,406 feet (1,343 meters), is Britain's highest peak. The Central Lowlands is a flatter area, with farms, **industries**, and most of the country's people. The large cities of Edinburgh and Glasgow are located there. In the hilly Southern Uplands, Cheviot Hills forms the border with England.

Above: The city of Perth is located on the River Tay, which is Scotland's longest river.

Climate

Although Scotland is near the Arctic Circle, the warm Gulf Stream in the North Atlantic helps keep winters mild. Average winter temperatures are 37° to 41° Fahrenheit (2.8° to 5° Celsius). Summers are cool, with temperatures averaging only about 59° F (15° C). Western Scotland is usually warmer and wetter than eastern Scotland.

Plants and Animals

Hardy plants, such as mosses, grow well in Scotland's northern Highlands.

Below: Eilean Donan Castle, built near Dornie in 1260, has a covering of snow in winter.

Left: Puffins nest on rocky cliffs along the western coast of the Highlands.

Grasses, **heather**, and wildflowers cover the central and southern areas. Among the country's few trees, oaks and **conifers** are the most common.

Of the animals native to Scotland, only Shetland ponies and shaggy, long-horned cattle still roam freely through the Highlands. Red deer, which are the largest wild animals in Britain, roam the Highlands, too. Golden eagles and buzzards fly over Scotland's mountain areas, and about half of the world's gray seals **breed** in Scottish waters.

History

The Picts were ancient inhabitants of Scotland. In A.D. 43, this fierce, warlike tribe successfully drove back Roman invaders, who had already conquered England. The Picts kept the Romans from adding Caledonia, which is what the ancient Romans called Scotland, to their empire.

Above: The Picts of northern and central Scotland were the country's most powerful tribe. They painted and tattooed their bodies to frighten their enemies.

In the eleventh century, Britons from the south, Scots from Ireland, and Angles from northern Europe joined the Picts to form the nation known as Scotland. Traditionally, the people of Scotland belonged to different tribes or **clans**. Each clan had its own chief, and its people were deeply loyal.

The Stuarts

From 1371 to 1714, the Stuarts ruled Scotland. In the late 1500s, a rivalry between two royal cousins, Scotland's Queen Mary Stuart (r. 1542–1567) and England's Queen Elizabeth I (r. 1558–

Left: Scotland had a **feudal system** of government in the twelfth century. Landlords charged people money to live and work on their land. In this picture, a worker is paying money to his landlord.

1603), ended with Mary's execution in 1587. When Elizabeth died without an heir, Mary's son, who ruled Scotland, also became the legal heir to England's throne. In Scotland, he remained King James VI. In England, he was James I. Since that time, England's **monarch** has also ruled Scotland.

Union with England

In 1707, the governments of England and Scotland united, making Scotland part of the United Kingdom. Many Highland Scots were against this union and formed the Jacobite army to fight for Scottish independence. The final defeat of the Jacobite army came in 1746 at the Battle of Culloden.

The Industrial Revolution

Scotland was an agricultural country until the eighteenth century, when

Below:
By the end of the nineteenth century, Glasgow was a center of industry and a major port for trade and travel.

many farmers moved to the cities to work in industries such as textiles, shipbuilding, iron casting, and coal mining. Those who stayed on farms became very poor, and some finally left Scotland to live in other countries.

Above:
A bagpiper leads Scottish soldiers along a road in France during World War I.

World War I

When World War I broke out in 1914, many Scots went to France to fight, and many died. After the war ended, in 1918, Scotland suffered a severe economic **depression**.

Home Rule

During the 1920s, economic problems in Scotland continued to grow. Some people thought the country would be better off independent. The Scottish Nationalist Party (SNP) was formed in 1928 to work toward self-government, but it had little success. In 1979, a vote for home rule also failed. In 1999, however, with the support of British prime minister Tony Blair, a new Scottish **Parliament** opened. Donald Dewar was its First Minister.

Below:
Queen Elizabeth II (*second from right*) and Prince Philip, Duke of Edinburgh (*second from left*), join Donald Dewar (*center*) at the 1999 opening of the new Scottish Parliament.

Elsie Maude Inglis (1864–1917)

Women's rights supporter Elsie Maude Inglis was a Scottish doctor. During World War I, she helped set up the Organization of Scottish Women's Hospitals. After she died, the Elsie Inglis Maternity Hospital in Edinburgh was built in her honor.

Elsie Maude Inglis

John Knox (c. 1514–1572)

A religious reformer who supported the Protestant movement, John Knox established the Presbyterian Church in Scotland.

John Knox

Alexander Fleming (1881–1955)

The brilliant scientist Alexander Fleming was the son of a Scottish sheep farmer. In 1928, he discovered *penicillin*, which has been used ever since to treat many different diseases. Fleming was awarded the Nobel Prize for Medicine in 1945.

Alexander Fleming

Government and the Economy

With the establishment of the Scottish Parliament in 1999, Scotland now acts independently on matters of housing, health care, and other important issues that directly affect the Scottish people. Scotland's parliament has 129 elected members and is located in Edinburgh.

As part of the United Kingdom, Scotland also has 72 ministers who represent the country in the British

Left: Members of the Scottish Parliament were sworn in at the parliament's first session in Edinburgh on May 12, 1999.

Parliament's House of Commons. Scotland's secretary of state helps settle any differences that arise between Scottish interests and the government of the United Kingdom.

Below:
The Scottish Office building, located in Edinburgh, was specially designed to make good use of natural light. The building was completed in 1996.

THE SCOTTISH OFFICE

The Legal System

Scotland's legal system has its roots in ancient Roman law. Its highest court, the Court of Session, takes care of **civil** matters. Criminal cases are heard by a judge and jury in the High Court of Justiciary. Sheriff courts deal with less serious civil and criminal cases.

The Economy

Agriculture has been part of Scotland's economy for hundreds of years, and about one-fourth of the land is still used for farming. The most important crops are wheat, barley, and potatoes. Scotland is also known for its high-quality beef cattle and dairy products. Fishing is another important industry. Scotland provides more than two-thirds of the fish and shellfish in the United Kingdom's total annual catch.

Below: Most of the small island of Iona is rough grazing land for sheep and cattle.

Above:
What was once a
carpet factory is now
a modern business
center in Glasgow.

Since the economic depression that followed World War I, Scotland has moved away from heavy industry such as coal mining and iron casting. With the discovery of oil and natural gas in the North Sea, however, Aberdeen has become one of Europe's major **petrochemical** centers. Glasgow is an important seaport, as well as a center for high-technology industries. Electronics and computer software are among Scotland's main exports.

People and Lifestyle

Hardworking Scots are known for their honesty, sense of humor, and national pride, and the country has a rich mixture of cultures and races.

Below: This **croft** is in Balallan on Lewis Island. **Peat** is piled up outside the house to be used as fuel during the winter months.

Along with Europeans, people from India, Pakistan, Southeast Asia, New Zealand, and North America have come to live and work in Scotland.

When social changes in the 1700s and 1800s combined small farms into large estates, many Scottish farmers were forced to leave their land and find new homes. Some stayed in rural areas and became crofters. Others moved to cities in the Central Lowlands, to work in the factories, or to countries such as the United States and Canada.

Today, even with Scotland's high level of employment, many Scots are poor. Although the growth of tourism has helped Scotland's rural economy, about one-third of the people in rural areas live in poverty and do not have decent housing.

Above: This boy and his grandfather are taking a walk in the Highlands. Both are wearing traditional Scottish clothing.

Family Life

Families are important to the Scots. Parents, children, and grandparents often live together in the same house. Scots are very proud of their **heritage**, too, with parents passing on to their children the traditions, songs, and dances of Scotland. Parents also teach their children traditional values, such as the importance of education, hard work, courtesy, and respect.

Below: Families enjoy spending time together, even just walking along a stream on a sunny day.

Women in Scotland

In the 1800s, many Scottish women had jobs in the fish-processing and textile industries. Today, Scottish women have jobs in shops, banks, and restaurants. Many are educated at universities and work as teachers, doctors, and lawyers, and over one-third of Scottish Parliament members are women. Still, more women than men in Scotland live in poverty.

Above:
This factory worker in the city of Dundee is operating a loom. She is weaving a type of soft wool, called cashmere, that is often used to make sweaters.

Education

Scotland has long been recognized for the high-quality education it provides. All children between the ages of five and sixteen must go to school. Public schools are free, and parents play an active role in deciding school policies.

Students in Scotland must attend elementary school for seven years and junior high school for four years. In the last year of junior high, they take an examination to earn the Scottish Certificate of Education, or Standard

Left:
These students on the island of Skye are on their way home from school.

Left: The University of Saint Andrews dates back to 1411. It is the oldest of Scotland's fourteen universities.

Grade. Those who pass go on to one or two years of senior high school. More examinations are taken in senior high before a student can attend a college or university.

Scotland has twenty-three colleges and universities. Students can earn a three-year ordinary degree or a four-year honors degree. Students who do not attend a university often enroll in job-related training programs.

Left: This stained glass window of Saint Columba is in Iona Abbey. Saint Columba came to Scotland from Ireland and built a monastery on the island of Iona, off the west coast of Scotland.

Religion

The **Celtic** Saint Ninian first brought Christianity to Scotland in the fifth century. About a hundred years later, in 563, Saint Columba settled on the tiny island of Iona and worked to **convert** the Celtic tribes. By the eleventh century, however, Roman Catholicism was starting to replace Celtic Christianity as the main religion of Scotland.

Scotland broke away from Roman Catholicism in the 1500s as the result of a religious movement known as the Protestant Reformation. Led by a man named John Knox, this movement helped establish Presbyterianism in Scotland. The Presbyterian Church of Scotland is still the country's official religion. About 20 percent of Scots belong to the Church of Scotland, and about 15 percent are Roman Catholics.

Below: Glasgow Cathedral, built in 1508, is one of the few cathedrals of the Middle Ages that survived the Reformation.

Language

Almost everyone in Scotland today speaks English, the country's official language. Two other languages are *Gaelic*, spoken mostly by people in the Highlands, and *Scots*, or *Lallans* (LAH-lanz), which can be heard in southern Scotland.

Gaelic is a Celtic language related to Irish and Welsh. Scots, although similar to English, has Old English and Norse words that are not found in other varieties of English.

Left: The city of Edinburgh's Holyrood Park is a nice place to relax outdoors in autumn.

Literature

Some of the world's finest writers and poets are Scottish. Robert Louis Stevenson (1850–1894) is famous for his classic adventure novel *Treasure Island*. Robert Burns (1759–1796) turned traditional folk songs of country life into great poetry. James Matthew Barrie (1860–1937) wrote *Peter Pan*, and Arthur Conan Doyle (1859–1930) created the world's greatest detective, Sherlock Holmes.

Above:
Robert Burns (*left*), Scotland's national poet, wrote lyrics for popular tunes such as *Auld Lang Syne*, a traditional song for New Year's Eve. Sir Walter Scott (1771–1832) (*right*) wrote *Rob Roy*, *Ivanhoe*, and other historical novels.

Arts

Music

The music of Scotland reflects the country's history and culture. Scottish ballads, such as "Loch Lomond," are one kind of traditional Scottish music. *Ceilidh* (KAY-lee) is also traditional music. It usually involves dancing and is often played at celebrations such as weddings. The popular band Runrig sings in Gaelic and uses traditional instruments, such as accordions and bagpipes, along with electric guitars

Left: Scotland's Evelyn Glennie is a classical musician. She has won many awards, including a Grammy in 1988, as a solo percussionist. The fact that Glennie is completely deaf makes her musical achievements even more impressive.

and drums in its modern rock style. Other Scottish rock bands include Wet, Wet, Wet and Simple Minds.

Above: The drone of bagpipes often accompanies a traditional Highland dance. These three "wee lassies" (little girls) are dancing at a street celebration in Edinburgh.

Dancing

Scottish dancing dates back to the 1200s. Traditional Highland dances require so much concentration and skill that they were often used to train soldiers for battle. Both country and ceilidh dancing follow strict routines performed to live music.

Architecture

Scotland's landscape is dotted with the hill forts, **crannogs**, and **brochs** of the Bronze and Iron Ages and the castles, churches, and monasteries of the Middle Ages.

Heavy, Gothic styles of British architecture in the nineteenth century gave way, in the twentieth century, to more modern forms, such as "the Glasgow Style," introduced by Charles Rennie Mackintosh (1868–1928).

Below:
Floors Castle in the Southern Uplands is the home of the Duke and Duchess of Roxburghe. It was built in 1721 and modified in the nineteenth century.

Left:
Scottish architects
Charles Rennie
Mackintosh and
Margaret MacDonald,
who were married to
each other, designed
their Glasgow home,
where they lived
from 1906 to 1914.

This distinctive style mixed traditional
Scottish architecture with Japanese art
and **art nouveau**. Modern architecture
in Scotland today features glass and
geometric designs.

Painting

Four Glasgow artists, known as
"the Scottish Colourists," received
worldwide praise for their use of bold,
vivid colors. Samuel Peploe (1871–
1935), John Fergusson (1874–1961),
George Hunter (1877–1931), and
Francis Caddell (1883–1937) still
influence young artists today.

Leisure

Scots like to get together with family and friends. They also enjoy outdoor activities, such as going for walks in the country. Some hike on the many footpaths and trails that crisscross the **moors** of the Central Lowlands, but hill walking is also very popular. It involves **trekking** up a mountain that is over 3,000 feet (914 m) high. Scotland has 284 of these mountains.

Left: The Ramblers Association and other hiking clubs in Scotland try to make sure that the country's footpaths and hiking trails are open for walkers to use all year long.

Because Scotland has many rivers, lakes, and streams, fishing is another very popular activity. The country is world famous for its salmon. The best rivers for salmon fishing in Scotland are the Tay and the Dee.

Above: Scots enjoy eating and relaxing at outdoor cafés in nice weather.

Popular indoor activities for Scots include reading, watching television, listening to music, and playing board games — or bingo!

Sports

The people of Scotland are enthusiastic sports fans. Soccer is so popular that almost every town and village has its own team. The country's most famous teams are the Celtic Football Club and the Rangers Football Club. Both of these clubs are from Glasgow.

Golf is a sport that actually started in Scotland, where it was played as early as the fifteenth century. The country has over four hundred golf courses, including the Royal and Ancient Golf Club of St. Andrews.

Below: St. Andrews, in the Fife region, is recognized around the world as the "Home of Golf."

Along with soccer, golf, rugby, and other popular sports, Scots also have their traditional sports. Shinty is an ancient Celtic sport that is played with a stick and a ball. Curling is a winter sport in Scotland that dates back to the early sixteenth century.

Left:
Curling is played on ice. Players use brooms, or brushes, to push round, flat stones toward a circle, called a button. The team with its stones closest to the button wins.

Below:
Jackie Stewart, "the Flying Scot," has won three World Drivers Championships.

Formula One Racing

Scotland's Jackie Stewart is one of the most famous names in car racing history. He won twenty-seven Grand Prix races in his Formula One career.

Festivals

Each year, Edinburgh hosts two world-famous arts festivals. The Edinburgh Military Tattoo is a music festival that draws international bagpipe and drum bands to Edinburgh Castle in August. At about the same time, the Edinburgh International Festival is presenting its drama, opera, and concerts.

Most Scottish towns and villages offer at least one local festival each year. Clan gatherings and Highland

Below: A bagpipe band is lined up outside Edinburgh Castle, ready to march and play.

Games are among the most popular local celebrations. Featured events include traditional Scottish sports and Highland dancing.

Above: Performers from the Edinburgh International Festival parade through the streets in costumes.

Hogmanay is a popular New Year celebration. It is an ancient holiday when people traditionally take gifts of oatmeal cakes to relatives and friends to bring them good luck. At Halloween, on October 31, Scottish children dress in costumes and go door to door asking for treats.

Food

Scottish food is simple, but tasty. The Scots enjoy a variety of meats, including Aberdeen Angus beef, venison, lamb, and **grouse**. Fish is also a favorite food. Salmon, trout, shrimp, mussels, and lobsters can all be found in Scottish waters.

Other popular foods are Scotch broth; stovied tatties, an onion and potato dish; and bannocks, which are barley and oat biscuits.

Left: Shellfish are popular foods, especially in Scotland's coastal towns and villages.

Haggis is a Scottish **delicacy**. It is a type of sausage made of sheep **entrails**, oats, pepper, and onions, sewn into a sheep's stomach bag and boiled.

Left:
People either love or hate the taste of haggis. This butcher shop has uncooked haggis hanging in its front window.

Eating in Scotland

A traditional Scottish breakfast can be porridge, oatcakes, or a hearty plateful of sausage, bacon, eggs, and potato scones. Scots eat another cooked meal at about 5:00 p.m. The evening meal is eaten late, sometimes after 9:00 p.m. Pizza places are popular in Scotland, as fast food becomes more common.

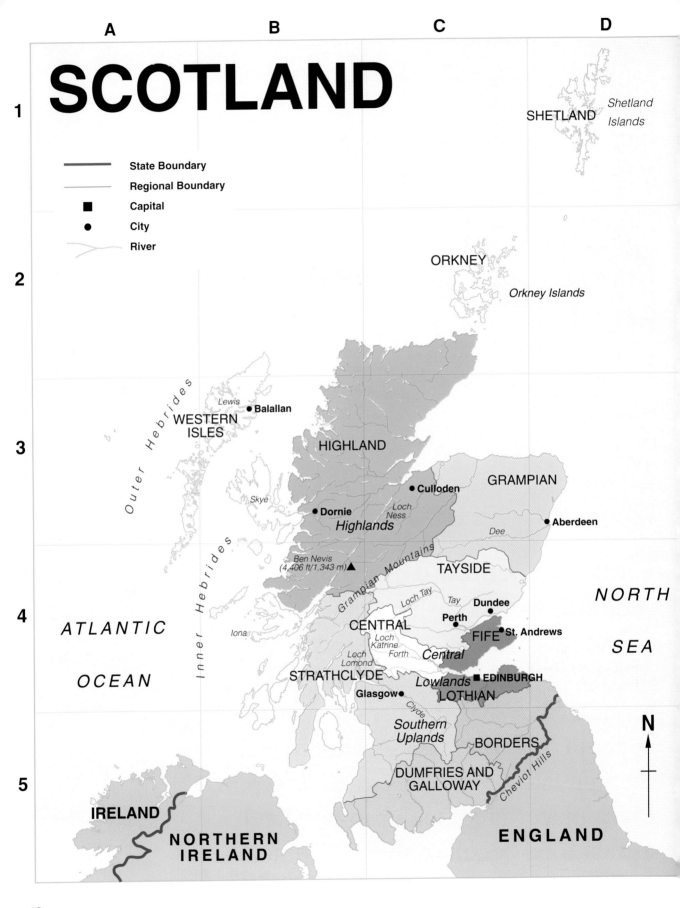

SCOTLAND

State Boundary
Regional Boundary
■ Capital
● City
River

SHETLAND — *Shetland Islands*

ORKNEY — *Orkney Islands*

WESTERN ISLES

Lewis ● Balallan

Outer Hebrides

HIGHLAND

GRAMPIAN

Skye

● Culloden

Loch Ness

● Dornie

Highlands

● Aberdeen

Dee

Ben Nevis
(4,406 ft/1,343 m) ▲

Grampian Mountains

TAYSIDE

Loch Tay

Tay

● Dundee

● Perth

CENTRAL

FIFE

● St. Andrews

Inner Hebrides

Iona

Loch Katrine

Forth

Central

ATLANTIC

OCEAN

Loch Lomond

STRATHCLYDE

Lowlands

■ EDINBURGH

LOTHIAN

Glasgow ●

Clyde

Southern Uplands

BORDERS

NORTH

SEA

N

DUMFRIES AND GALLOWAY

Cheviot Hills

IRELAND

NORTHERN IRELAND

ENGLAND

Above: Scotland's scenic mountains are great places to ski.

Aberdeen D3
Atlantic Ocean
    A5–D1

Balallan B3
Ben Nevis B4
Borders Region
    C4–D5

Central Lowlands
    B4–C4
Central Region C4
Cheviot Hills C5–D5
Culloden C3

Dornie B3
Dumfries and
    Galloway Region
    B5–C5
Dundee C4

Edinburgh C4
England C5–D5

Fife Region C4

Glasgow C4
Grampian Mountains
    B4–C4
Grampian Region
    C3–D4

Highland Region
    B2–C4
Highlands B2–C4

Inner Hebrides
    Islands B3–B4
Iona Island B4
Ireland A5
Island of Skye B3

Lewis Island B2–B3
Loch Katrine C4
Loch Lomond
    B4–C4
Loch Ness C3

Loch Tay C4
Lothian Region C4

North Sea D2–D5
Northern Ireland
    A5–B5

Orkney Islands C2
Outer Hebrides
    Islands A4–B2

Perth C4

River Clyde C4–C5

River Dee C4–D3
River Forth C4
River Tay C4

St. Andrews C4
Shetland Islands D1
Southern Uplands C5
Strathclyde Region
    B4–C5

Tayside Region C4

Western Isles A4–B2

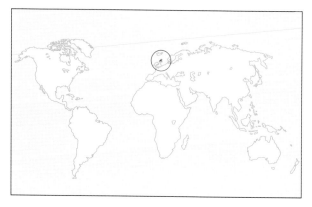

Quick Facts

Official Name	Scotland (part of the United Kingdom of Great Britain and Northern Ireland)
Capital	Edinburgh
Official Language	English
National Languages	Gaelic, Scots
Population	5.1 million (2001 estimate)
Land Area	30,418 square miles (78,783 square km)
Regions	Borders, Central, Dumfries and Galloway, Fife, Grampian, Highland, Lothian, Strathclyde, Tayside
Island Groups	Orkney, Shetland, Western Isles
Highest Point	Ben Nevis 4,406 feet (1,343 m)
Major Rivers	Clyde, Forth, Tay
Major Religions	Presbyterian Church of Scotland, Roman Catholic
Major Lakes	Loch Katrine, Loch Lomond, Loch Ness, Loch Tay
Major Cities	Aberdeen, Edinburgh, Glasgow
Currency	Pound Sterling (£0.70 = U.S. $1 in 2002)

Opposite: Edinburgh Castle towers over this ornate garden fountain.

45

Glossary

art nouveau: a design style that features flower and leaf designs with graceful curving lines.

breed: give birth to young.

brochs: round stone towers from the first century A.D. that are found only in Scotland.

Celtic: having to do with the early inhabitants of the British Isles.

civil: having to do with private arguments between people, rather than with criminal matters.

clans: groups of families that all have the same ancestors.

conifers: cone-bearing evergreen trees and shrubs, such as pine and spruce.

convert: change from one religious belief to another.

crannogs: small artificial islands that were built in many of the lakes of Scotland and Ireland and were strengthened for defense.

croft: a small field next to a house that is owned or rented by the person who farms the land.

delicacy: an uncommon food that is considered a luxury.

depression: a period of poor economic activity when people cannot find jobs and money is scarce.

entrails: the inside organs of an animal, such as its intestines.

feudal system: a kind of government in the Middle Ages in which people received land and protection from the owner of the land if they worked and fought for that person.

grouse: a small, fat bird of the pheasant family, which is hunted for food.

heather: an evergreen shrub that grows wild on the moors of Europe, and which is covered with clusters of tiny, pinkish purple flowers and has needlelike leaves closely attached to its stalks.

heritage: the customs and traditions that have belonged to a group of people for a long time.

industries: businesses that manufacture goods in factories.

inhabited: occupied by people.

monarch: a king or queen.

moors: large, open areas of swampy grasslands commonly found in England and Scotland.

parliament: a group of people elected to make a country's laws.

peat: partly rotted plants in swampy areas that have formed a dark, soil-like substance which, when dried, can be used as fuel.

petrochemical: a chemical that comes from natural oil or gas.

trekking: walking a long distance across hills and mountains.

More Books to Read

Alexander Fleming and the Story of Penicillin. John Bankston (Mitchell Lane)

Favorite Celtic Fairy Tales. Joseph Jacobs (Dover)

The History of Scotland for Children. Judy Paterson (Gloworm)

Letters Home from Scotland. Marcia S. Gresko (Blackbirch Marketing)

A Little Book of Scottish Quotations. J. D. Sutherland (Appletree Press)

Little House in the Highlands. Melissa Wiley (HarperCollins Children's Books)

Scotland. Faces and Places series. Marycate O'Sullivan (Child's World)

Scotland. Festivals of the World series. Jonathan Griffiths (Gareth Stevens)

A Visit to the United Kingdom. Rachael Bell (Heinemann Library)

Whuppity Stoorie: A Scottish Folk Tale. Carolyn White (GP Putnam)

Videos

Castles of Scotland. (Acorn Media)

Scotland . . . Beauty and Majesty. (BFS Entertainment & Multimedia)

Scotland the Brave. (Acorn Media)

William Wallace. (Kultur Video)

Web Sites

www.darkisle.com

www.geo.ed.ac.uk/home/scotland/scotland.html

www.infoplease.kids.lycos.com/ce6/world/A0844104.htm

www.scotland.gov.uk/pages/news/junior/

Due to the dynamic nature of the Internet, some web sites stay current longer than others. To find additional web sites, use a reliable search engine with one or more of the following keywords to help you locate information about Scotland. Keywords: *bagpipes, croft, Edinburgh, Gaelic, Glasgow, haggis, Highland Games, kilts, St. Andrews, Scottish clans.*

Index

Aberdeen 19
agriculture 12, 18
animals 8, 9
architecture 32, 33
arts 30, 33, 38
Atlantic Ocean 6, 8

bagpipes 13, 30, 31, 38
Barrie, James
    Matthew 29
Ben Nevis 7
Britain 6, 7, 9, 16, 32
Burns, Robert 29

castles 8, 32, 38
Central Lowlands 6,
    7, 21, 34
Cheviot Hills 7
clans 10, 38
climate 8

dancing 22, 30, 31, 39
Dewar, Donald 14
Doyle, Arthur Conan 29
Dundee 23

economy 13, 14, 16, 18,
    19, 21
Edinburgh 5, 7, 14, 15,
    16, 17, 28, 31, 38, 39
education 22, 23, 24, 25
England 6, 7, 10, 11, 12
exports 19

families 22, 34
farming 7, 13, 15, 18, 20
festivals 38, 39
fishing 18, 23, 35
flag 5
Fleming, Alexander 15
food 40, 41

Gaelic 5, 28, 30
Glasgow 7, 12, 19, 27,
    32, 33, 36
Glennie, Evelyn 30
government 11, 12, 14,
    16, 17

haggis 41
Highlands 7, 8, 9, 12, 21,
    28, 31, 38, 39

independence 12, 14, 16
industries 7, 12, 13, 18,
    19, 23
Inglis, Elsie Maude 15
Iona 18, 26
Ireland 6, 10, 26
islands 6, 18, 20, 24, 26

kilts 5
Knox, John 15, 27

language 28
law 17

leisure 34, 35
literature 29

mountains 7, 9, 34
music 30, 31, 35, 38

North Sea 6, 19

parliament 14, 16, 23
Perth 7
Picts 10
plants 8, 9

religion 15, 26, 27
rivers 6, 7, 35

Saint Andrew 5, 25
St. Andrews 36
Scott, Sir Walter 29
Southern Uplands 7, 32
sports 36, 37, 39
Stevenson, Robert
    Louis 29
Stewart, Jackie 37
Stuarts 10

United Kingdom 5, 6,
    12, 16, 17, 18

Wales 6
women 15, 23
World War I 13, 15, 19